Already Becoming

poems

Zoa Coudret

Harvard Square Press
Cambridge, Massachusetts

2022 © Zoa Coudret
All Rights Reserved

Harvard Square Press
Cambridge, MA
United States of America
ISBN: 9798425090065
Cover Image: *Mann og kvinne inne i en ring*, bronze,
Gustav Vigeland, 1930-1931, Frognerparken, Oslo.
Photo by Zoa Coudret.

Harvard Square Press
Cambridge, Massachusetts

harvardsquarepress.com

Already Becoming

CONTENTS

"Climb up on the Moon? Of course we did. All you had to do was row out to it in a boat and, when you were underneath, prop a ladder against her and scramble up."

— From "The Distance of the Moon" by Italo Calvino

"Tonight, let us praise our mothers of extinction,
mothers of miscarriage, mothers of cheap nature,
pray for us, because even tomorrow will be haunted…"

— From "Halloween in the Anthropocene" by Craig Santos Perez

Home

If a young enby falls
asleep in the forest, do they have
a gender?

They rub their face
across mossy rocks
like a cat upon an armchair,
how can you call them
boy or *girl* and not *cascade*
of extrahuman combustion?

They are nostalgic for somersaults
in fields full of buttery weeds,
elliptical swarms of starlings
over cattails, it's called
a murmuration but memory
renders it silent.

Home was where their feet grew
into the floor like coral, reefed
in with their saw-toothed family, where
they opened their mouth and ate plankton
just to survive as satellites transmitted
different ways of being, translucent,
primordial. They escaped only when
they writhed enough, gashed
enough at their maladaptive body
so that it became
something true.

Desires are already memories

Do you remember the boundless Venetian waters,
        washing over the streets like baptismal fonts
                run amok? Someone should write new fables

where gondolas float over St. Mark's Square,
        and the wealthy locals commute in palanquins
                above the floods while tourists drown.

Or is it too soon for stories based on the real
        apocalypse? We carry them in us, anyway,
                votive offerings to a failing order. Maybe

I'm a little eager for disaster to come, to be
        done with this impending-catastrophe life.
                In my spare time, I record temperatures,

ever rising, for the weather service and pick
        wildflowers where meadowlarks no longer fly.
                My hand reaches out, feeling for spiderwebs

while foraging mushrooms in a half-cut forest.
        At night, I train astrolabe skyward to map the bodies
                hurtling toward Earth, though I've seen none yet.

How can we be happy at the center of concentric
        dystopias? Here in the metropolis, I shout and shout,
                but it is still too pleasant to live, too easy to forget.

A single point

I arrive here, hurled
through space and time
with a velocity I can't control,
becoming trans, bumping into people
I don't want to touch, greeting neighbors
whose names I will never know.

I dream of grazing the fields
alone, gossiping with wheat, milling
my own flour and kneading bread
with these useless hands, but my
colonizer ancestors dismantled
the common lands in their
genocidal outburst, an expansion
of cruelty shrouded in god's love.

I took off my halo long ago.

They say Andromeda
and the Milky Way will collide,
form one galaxy, I bet neither
wants to share space in the universe,
that's why those who live there
have sent no signals to greet us yet.

When I look up at the punctiform light
of the stars, I don't see beauty,
I see violence, I see accidental explosions
and implosions, all the isotopes
of all the elements falling
back together to reform
at one greedy point.

The way we lived

1.

You said you were shapeless
before we kissed, a nebula

trying to emerge from darkness.
I didn't believe you, licked

velvety dust from your shoulders
until I felt the cold metallic plate

underneath, where cutaneous
layers should have been.

When I told you my secret,
you made me recount

meaningless memories to prove
my queerness, as if it were a lab test

you wanted me to fail. You who
cauterized my wounds with lies,

disingenuous *I love you*s,
and thought I wouldn't notice

the quiet eruptions; I didn't,
until it was too late.

2.

Now I realize my own body
lacked form, a grainy sketch

of a person, until the cataclysm
of our love transmitted the truth

to me about myself: *You are not a man*,
I heard your fingers say, but after,

your lips told me, *You are a man.*
You must be a man. And because

the galactic possibilities of gender
were new to me, I trusted you.

3.

I trusted you and you found
the sensitive skin of my breast

and prodded it with your finger-
nail blades—my great-grandmother

had a heart-shaped pincushion,
I remember, and when she caught me

in her sewing room, she warned me
not to play with hearts or sharp objects,

but I thought she was just making a joke.

4.

I thought you were joking.

5.

I was never joking.

Already becoming

1.

I was already becoming
myself before I knew
who I could be, my family
must think there is a void
in the space the old me
occupied, or a parallel me
who went on writhing
in that barren life.

But it's not like I died.

I tell them the new me
was always there, signaling
a future of indefinite trans-
mission. I heralded this
in gestures even I couldn't
understand, polishing
pearl strings before I knew
I would ever wear them.

Look at me, as I plunge
deeper into myself;
this impalpable stuff
that we call human,
bulges out of my guts,
soft and unfathomable.

2.

When I make a schematic
of my life, I draw a skyscraper
zigzagging into clouds,
no symmetry governs life,
why should I try to align myself
with the groundwork already laid?
You call it a foundation, I call it
brainwashing. My body
won't obey the blueprints
you created for me.
Every day I blurt

out new labels that feel
right, and each day the echoes
haunt me, but it's fine,

it's fine, there's always
risk of ricochet when you
take a shot. The worst thing
is to be safe and motionless,
to hear your moans echo
in solitude.

3.

I must have been formed
underground like a turnip.
When I was young, I thought
they were called "turn-ups"
because that's what you did
to harvest them. And I wondered
why carrots and potatoes
didn't have such interesting names.

There was an indentation upon a hill
deep in the forest behind my childhood home,
where I would lie for hours, staring through
branches chandeliered above me.
When I was there, subterranean soil cooling
my back, I never needed to explain
myself, never needed to choose
pink or blue, boy or girl, skirt or pants.

The soil I turned with dirty hands
held me just the same.

Certain places

There are certain places I can't be me:
the restaurant patio overlooking the lake,

the factory where my hands accumulate calluses
& grease, the theme park where coasters extract screams.

I can't wear dresses anywhere but the cement
cage that is my apartment, exposed drainpipes

& other industrial filigree accept me. Sometimes
I put on lipstick & eyeshadow & walk

the cobblestone street over cellar doors,
drainage grates, other entrances to the underworld,

& dream of being light & shapeful as the clouds.

Filters

I want to be thin & pretty
but I have stared
at too many mirrors,

seen enchantments
on phone screens that
warp the body into something

sparkly & unreal.
Finger taps transform
my face, plumping

lips, narrowing
jawline, blushing
cheeks, but no one

will see me like this
off the internet.
Maybe I'll stay

in group chats & picture
feeds for the rest of my life,
show only the flattering

side of my filtered face,
wash my melancholies
down the shower drain,

pipes transporting
tears & sweat & blood
through walls & sewers,

far away from the carpets
& cushions where I snap
selfies & record videos

for my followers who
will never see this
hermetic catastrophe.

At a precise moment

I was only a child, 10 years old
        when I knew my atoms were

wrong, vintage carbon
        hesitant & expired.

I tiptoed out of the house
        & into pine trees, painted

the bark with my saliva,
        perfumed my pits with sap,

stripped naked & tucked
        my penis between my legs

& felt whole, laid in piles of leaves
        until I became used to how they itched.

Feedbacks

Sometimes I think no one cares
enough to shatter me,

so I scatter myself across
cybernetic entanglements,

a perpetual crucible where
I am formed and reformed,

instinctive quibbling
at the cellular level,

swelling like a burst
ellipsoid, a Caesar

dethroned, searching for stasis
across the wispy grasses of Elysium.

Before forming

What is luxury when
the atmosphere is dying,

      when the murderous oceans
      turn their fury toward land,

           when meteors break the crust?

I dream of the molten layers
of earth yawning open

      exposing the restful
      strata to a fiery climate.

           Before forming,

Earth's minerals huddled
together in stars.

      Before seclusion,
      the anchorite took one last look

           at the serpentine mosaic
           outside their cell

                and remembered each
                ceramic shard, its precise

                    position, until they felt
                    their heart's last palpitation,

                        a twitch in their chest.

Sometimes, I try
to remember who I was

      before I was born.

Without boundaries

I am small, can I still contain
multitudes?

> When you fail, a friend told me once,
> you must clear your eye-dust, mullet your hair,
> and cloak your glands with a sexy new outfit.

Sometimes my guts shudder when I consider
how I only love narcissists and know
they will never love me. Sometimes I retreat into myself,
fantasize that I am a mollusk, bird grub waiting
to be splatted on an embankment next to the sea.

> Imagine if ganglia
> were attached to antennae
> shooting out of our heads
> and our retinas could see
> as well as the mantis shrimp.
> Maybe then we could escape
> our Neolithic bodies,
> maybe then we could exist
> without boundaries.

Away from us

The Hubble Space Telescope
has been orbiting earth
longer than you have been alive,
and seven months less than me.
I wonder how many times
it sailed around us, observing
the limitless logic of our
togetherness, and whether
it saw the signs we couldn't see.

I don't want to distance
myself from you anymore,
we exist in the same sphere,
together or not. Did you know
I presentimented love when I saw you
scrawling poems in your journal,
flannel sleeves rolled, revealing
tattoo peonies on your forearms,
before we knew each other's names?

If we have another nexus,
I will shutter my euphoria,
Drape a modest veil over the eye
of the telescope.

Descended

My ancestors are dinosaurs
and osseous worms

huddled in mausoleums formed
before the Cenozoic. They speak

in the shallows of the lagoon
where crocodiles chomp

and the gurgle of a spring
draws earth-creatures en masse,

a gathering of terrestrial kinship,
ancient and modern.

They reassure me, *Sweetie,*
gender was as expansive and fluid
before the last glaciation,
an upheaval that brought us
closer together and carved
up the earth like a knife over
the skin of someone like you,
someone in flesh that doesn't fit.

And I believe them over my more recent
predecessors because the alternative

is to believe there are only two ways
of being and god's cruelty is a weapon
the believers can use for sport.

Unable to adapt

Elders claw their way
to retirement, decadent
and careless, starving
the young, unaware
of the race to apocalypse.

A new migration begins,
wealth hoarders go north
and inland, away from
degendered carcasses left
fleshless by beaks and talons
after endless epidemics.

The poor cry treachery,
the rich tremble and retreat
into the splendor of vacation homes
near sacred caverns of people
their ancestors displaced.
Glaciers melt back
over scarred mountains.

Who could blame them
for not wanting to witness
our self-inflicted extinction?

Returning

The famine persists
from unscorched tundra
to the provincial capital,

prosperity nowhere
to be found, the skull
of the decapitated emperor,

picked clean long ago
by hungry beaks, impaled
and erected at the crossroads

of the old capital, became
the emblem of the new world,
a warning for travelers.

A stranger rows from the estuary
under smashed bridges, searching
for signs of the life she used to lead

in this place. The foreignness she finds
erases her desires. The buildings have
fallen, their serrated shells tear the sky.

She pulls a piece of smooth glass
from the river's edge, looks around,
and rows away.

Abandoned cities

After seasons end, the inhabitants
pack dried fruit and stand on their roofs

or office tower precipices, some climb ladders
that eclipse the boundary of sky and never look down

to the colorless streets where they once walked
every Sunday to grab lattes or mimosas.

                           Nobody knows where they all go.

New cities, maybe, where they can invent

new ways of forgetting their mistakes,
new games to fuck each other over.

Prophecy

The oracles told me
    a stranger would come
on the autumn equinox,
    by way of a leafy route
guarded by wolves, they didn't
    warn me it would be a black cat
freed from its isolated shelter,
    a prison high in the burning mountains
where pagan priests reign over
    scorched gardens and mill flour
with the bones of extinct animals
    each winter solstice.

At least, that's the vibe
    I get from the cat when he stares,
out the window, eyes fierce
    with wonder, at the theater
of the street, birds pecking
    at seeds, chipmunks hoarding
nuts, waiting for his chance
    to pounce.

Guardians of the dead

Marble figures
    crane their necks

to see bodies lowered
    into the ground, burials

camera-recorded because
    full families can't attend,

so many funerals
    in so short a time,

the dead stacked
    like library books

in makeshift morgues,
    coroners and morticians

working overtime while millions
    of the living can't pay their rent.

Swallows light upon
    a new gravestone, chirp

harplike for masked
    visitors who lay flowers

on fresh sod. The cracked-cloak
    statues hum along, unnoticed.

As I went past

The basalt tombs don't say
which corpses are queer,
or where the vampires sleep,

only vulgar fragments
of nearly forgotten lives
poke out of the ground
and they won't last millennia,
not even hundreds of years.

Teeth and noses and hands
will remain, though, anonymous
and tormented by their exclusion
as new signs mark the newer dead.

I memorize names and dates,
create sagas of gay history,
implementing pasts that ring true
to me, to my people, even if
those who once owned these
bones were straight.

Death is queer and trans,
just like life, just like vampires,
just like the eroded grooves
of engraved headstones that I trace
with chipped-lacquer nails.

I lie above someone's long-rotted
coffin on soft grass and watch
a thunderstorm overtake the sky,
eager to become something else.

I'm still thinking about when

we drank from copper rivers,
walked barefoot through
constellations of glass
beneath railroad trestles,
reliving the times
we made forbidden love
in your family's cabin,
chimney belching smoke,
and tattooed magnolias
up our limbs in permanent
remembrance of the way
we bloomed together
at the right time.

AUTHOR NOTES AND ACKNOWLEDGEMENTS

The poems in this collection were composed using lists of words I compiled from two books by Italo Calvino: *Cosmicomics* and *Invisible Cities*. Any similarities in phrasings or ideas that may be in here are coincidental, although some of the titles are borrowed from phrases in Calvino's stories. Thematically, Calvino's linking of astronomy and humanity proved to be a big influence, much more than I had expected, on the ideas about ecological collapse, queerness, and personal history I tried to express here through poetry.

"Without boundaries," "Certain places," and "Home" were published online by *en*gendered* in March 2022.

"As I went past" and "Feedbacks" were published by *Powders Press* in March 2022.

Please visit engenderedlitmag.com and powderspress.com to read more poems like them.

ABOUT THE AUTHOR

Zoa Coudret (they/she) is a fiction writer, poet, student, teacher, and devotee of literature. They write and read stories that challenge heteronormativity and explore the weird, messy complexities of existing as a human body. Although they are a Libra sun, they low-key identify more with their Scorpio moon placement. You can read their stories and poems in *Peach Mag*, *New South*, *Longleaf Review*, *The Lumiere Review*, *The Hallowzine*, and elsewhere. They are an MFA candidate in fiction at Northern Michigan University and work as an associate editor for *Passages North*.

PUBLISHER NOTES

The 2021 International 3-Day Poetry Chapbook Contest was made possible with generous support from the NEA Big Read, Peter White Public Library, and the Friends of Peter White Public Library.

<u>Winners</u>:
1st Place – *Our Natural Satellite* by Russell Brakefield
2nd Place – *Conjuring a Ghost & Other Ways to Ruin Your Teeth* by
                  Randi Clemens
3rd Place – *Already Becoming* by Zoa Coudret

<u>Judge</u>:
Cindy Hunter Morgan

Made in the USA
Middletown, DE
25 April 2022

64696999R00022